Irish Poems

A collection for children selected by
Fiona Waters

Illustrated by
Peter Rutherford

Gill & Macmillan

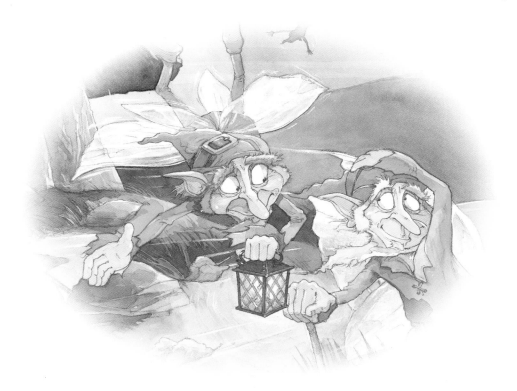

For Conor McMillen, with love

Acknowledgements

Padraic Colum The Old Woman of the Roads by permission of The Estate of Padraic Colum.

Seamus Heaney St Francis and the Birds from Death of a Naturalist by Seamus Heaney published by Faber and Faber, by permission of Seamus Heaney and by permission of Farrar, Straus & Giroux.

Patrick Kavanagh A Christmas Childhood part 1 Reprinted from Selected Poems, edited by Antoinette Quinn (Penguin Books, 1996) with permission of the Trustees of the Estate of the late Katherine B Kavanagh, through the Jonathan Williams Literary Agency.

Brendan Kennelly Girl in a Rope from Breathing Spaces: Early Poems by Brendan Kennelly, Bloodaxe Books, 1992.

Michael Longley The Meteorite from The Weather in Japan, Jonathan Cape, 2000. Used by permission of The Random House Group Limited.

Donagh MacDonagh A Poaching Song. Every effort has been made to trace the copyright holder without success. The publisher will be happy to rectify this omission in future reprints.

Derek Mahon Astronaut By permission of the author and The Gallery Press, Loughcrew, Oldcastle, Co. Meath, Ireland, from Derek Mahon Collected Poems, 1999.

Mary O'Malley Starting School from Where the Rocks Float, 1993 by permission of the author and Salmon Publishing, Knockeven, Cliffs of Moher, Co.Clare, Ireland.

W B Yeats The Song of Wandering Aengus by permission of A P Watt Ltd on behalf of Michael B Yeats.

This book was created by Tony Potter Publishing Ltd
Edited by Sheila Mortimer
Designed by Tony Potter

Published in Ireland by Gill & Macmillan Ltd
Hume Avenue, Park West, Dublin 12
www.gillmacmillan.ie
with associated companies throughout the world

© 2001 Tony Potter Publishing Ltd
ISBN 0-7171-3286-2
Printed by X-PRESS s.r.l.
Bound by Legatoria S. Tonti
NAPLES – ITALY

Contents

The Fairies in New Ross

When moonlight
Near midnight
Tips the rock and waving wood;
When moonlight
Near midnight
Silvers o'er the sleeping flood;
When yew-tops
With dew-drops
Sparkle o'er deserted graves;
'Tis then we fly
Through the welkin high,
Then we sail o'er the yellow waves.

Anonymous

4

All Things Bright and Beautiful

All things bright and beautiful,
All creatures great and small,
All things wise and wonderful,
The Lord God made them all.

Each little flower that opens,
Each little bird that sings,
He made their glowing colours,
He made their tiny wings.

The purple-headed mountain,
The river running by,
The sunset, and the morning,
That brightens up the sky;

The cold wind in the winter,
The pleasant summer sun,
The ripe fruits in the garden
He made them every one.

The tall trees in the greenwood,
The meadows where we play,
The rushes by the water
We gather every day.

He gave us eyes to see them,
And lips that we might tell,
How great is God Almighty,
Who has made all things well.

Cecil Frances Alexander

The Leprahaun

In a shady nook one moonlit night,
    A leprahaun I spied
In scarlet coat and cap of green,
    A cruiskeen by his side.
'Twas tick, tack, tick, his hammer went,
    Upon a weeny shoe,
And I laughed to think of a purse of gold,
    But the fairy was laughing too.

With tip-toe step and beating heart,
    Quite softly I drew nigh.
There was mischief in his merry face,
    A twinkle in his eye;
He hammered and sang with tiny voice,
    And sipped the mountain dew;
Oh! I laughed to think he was caught at last,
    But the fairy was laughing, too.

As quick as thought I grasped the elf,
    'Your fairy purse,' I cried,
'My purse?' said he, ' 'tis in her hand,
    That lady by your side.'
I turned to look, the elf was off,
    And what was I to do?
Oh! I laughed to think what a fool I'd been,
    And the fairy was laughing too.

Robert Dwyer Joyce

Cockles and Mussels

In Dublin's fair city,
Where the girls are so pretty,
    I first set my eyes on sweet Mollie Malone,
She wheeled her wheel-barrow
Through streets broad and narrow,
    Crying, 'Cockles and mussels, alive, alive, oh!'
      Alive, alive, oh! Alive, alive, oh!
      Crying, 'Cockles and mussels, alive, alive, oh!'

She was a fishmonger.
But sure 'twas no wonder,
    For so were her father and mother before.
And they both wheeled their barrow
Through streets broad and narrow,
    Crying, 'Cockles and mussels, alive, alive, oh!'
      Alive, alive, oh! Alive, alive, oh!
      Crying, 'Cockles and mussels, alive, alive, oh!'

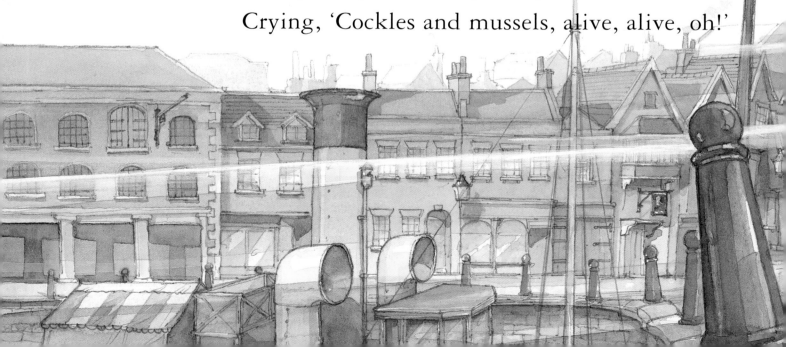

She died of a fever,
And none could relieve her,
	And that was the end of sweet Mollie Malone.
But her ghost wheels her barrow
Through streets broad and narrow,
	Crying, 'Cockles and mussels, alive, alive, oh!'
	Alive, alive, oh! Alive, alive, oh!
		Crying, 'Cockles and mussels,
			alive, alive, oh!'

Anonymous

Beasts and Birds

The dog will come when he is called,
The cat will walk away;
The monkey's cheek is very bald,
The goat is fond of play.
The parrot is a prate-apace,
Yet knows not what she says;
The noble horse will win the race,
Or draw you in a chaise.
The pig is not a feeder nice,
The squirrel loves a nut,
The wolf would eat you in a trice,
The buzzard's eyes are shut.
The lark sings high up in the air,
The linnet in the tree;
The swan he has a bosom fair,
And who so proud as he?

Adelaide O'Keeffe

A Bird is Calling From the Willow

A bird is calling from the willow
with lovely beak, a clean call.
Sweet yellow tip; he is black and strong.
It is doing a dance, the blackbird's song.

Anonymous

The Little Waves of Breffny

The grand road from the mountain goes shining
　　to the sea,
And there is traffic on it and many a horse
　　and cart,
But the little roads of Cloonagh are dearer
　　far to me,
And the little roads of Cloonagh go rambling
　　through my heart.

A great storm from the ocean goes shouting o'er
　　the hill,
And there is glory in it and terror on the wind,
But the haunted air of twilight is very strange
　　and still,
　　And the little winds of twilight are dearer to
　　　my mind.

14

The great waves of the Atlantic sweep storming
     on the way,
Shining green and silver with the hidden
     herring shoal,
But the Little Waves of Breffny have drenched
     my heart in spray.
And the Little Waves of Breffny go stumbling
     through my soul.

Eva Gore-Booth

The Old Woman of the Roads

Oh, to have a little house!
To own the hearth and stool and all!
The heaped-up sods upon the fire,
The pile of turf against the wall!

To have a clock with weights and chains
And pendulum swinging up and down,
A dresser filled with shining delph,
Speckled and white and blue and brown!

I could be busy all the day
Clearing and sweeping the hearth and floor,
And fixing on their shelf again
My white and blue and speckled store!

I could be quiet there at night
Beside the fire and by myself,
Sure of a bed and loath to leave
The ticking clock and the shining delph!

Och! but I'm weary of mist and dark,
And roads where there's never a house nor bush,
And tired I am of bog and road,
And the crying wind and the lonesome hush!

And I am praying to God on high,
And I am praying Him night and day,
For a little house, a house of my own –
Out of the wind's and the rain's way.

Padraic Colum

The Shadow People

Old Lame Brigid doesn't hear
Fairy music in the grass
When the gloaming's on the mere
And the shadow people pass:
Never hears their tiny feet
Coming from the village street
Just beyond the parson's wall,
Where the clover globes are sweet
And the mushroom's parasol
Opens in the moonlit rain.
Every night I hear them call
From their long and merry train.
Old Lame Brigid says to me
'It is just your fancy, child.'

She cannot believe I see
Laughing faces in the wild,
Hands that twinkle in the sedge
Bowing at the water's edge
Where the finny minnows quiver,
Shaping on a blue wave's edge
Bubble foam to sail the river.
And the sunny hands to me
Beckon ever, beckon ever.
Oh! I would be wild and free
And with the shadow people be.

Francis Ledwidge

19

My Aunt Jane

My aunt Jane, she took me in
She gave me tea out o' her wee tin
Half a bap and a wee snow top
And cinnamon buds out o' her wee shop.

My aunt Jane has a bell at the door
A white step-stone and a clean-swept floor
Candy-apples and hard green pears
And conversation lozengers.

My aunt Jane can dance a jig
And sing a ballad round a sweetie pig
Wee red eyes, and a cord for a tail
Hanging in a bunch from a farthing nail.

My aunt Jane, she's awful smart
She bakes a ring in an apple tart
And when that Hallow E'en comes around
Fornenst that tart I'm always found.

Anonymous

20

A Riddle

We are little airy creatures,
All of different voice and features,
One of us in glass is set,
One of us you'll find in jet,
T'other you may see in tin,
And the fourth a box within,
If the fifth you should pursue
It can never fly from you.

Jonathan Swift

Hold this up to a mirror to find the answer:
the vowels

The Wayfarer

The beauty of the world hath made me sad,
This beauty that will pass;
Sometimes my heart hath shaken with great joy
To see a leaping squirrel in a tree,
Or a red lady-bird upon a stalk,
Or little rabbits in a field at evening,
Lit by a slanting sun,
Or some green hill where shadows drifted by,
Some quiet hill where mountainy man hath sown
And soon will reap, near to the gate of Heaven;
Or children with bare feet upon the sands
Of some ebbed sea, or playing on the streets
Of little towns in Connacht,
Things young and happy.
And then my heart hath told me:
These will pass,
Will pass and change, will die and be no more,
Things bright and green, things young and happy;
And I have gone upon my way
Sorrowful.

Patrick Pearse

Herrings

Be not sparing,
Leave off swearing.
Buy my herring
Fresh from Malahide,
Better never was tried.
Come, eat them with pure fresh butter and mustard,
Their bellies are soft, and as white as a custard.
Come, sixpence a dozen, to get me some bread,
Or, like my own herrings, I soon shall be dead.

Jonathan Swift

6d
DOZEN

A Ballad of Master McGrath

Eighteen sixty nine being the date of the year,
Those Waterloo sportsmen and more did appear
For to gain the great prizes and bear them awa',
Never counting on Ireland and Master McGrath.

On the 12th of December, that day of renown,
McGrath and his keeper they left Lurgan town;
A gale in the Channel, it soon drove them o'er,
On the thirteenth they landed on fair England's shore.

And when they arrived there in big London town,
Those great English sportsmen they all gathered
   round –
And some of the gentlemen gave a 'Ha! Ha!'
Saying: 'Is that the great dog you call
   Master McGrath?'

And one of those gentlemen standing around
Says: 'I don't care a damn for your Irish
          greyhound';
And another he laughs with a scornful 'Ha! Ha!
We'll soon humble the pride of your Master
          McGrath.'

Then Lord Lurgan came forward and said:
  'Gentlemen,
If there's any amongst you has money to spend –
For you nobles of England I don't care a straw –
Here's five thousand to one upon Master
  McGrath.'

Then McGrath he looked up and he wagged his
  old tail,
Informing his lordship, 'I know what you mane,
Don't fear, noble Brownlow, don't fear them, agra,
For I'll tarnish their laurels,' says Master McGrath.

And Rose stood uncovered, the great English
  pride,
Her master and keeper were close by her side;
They have let her away and the crowd cried,
  'Hurrah!'
For the pride of all England – and Master
  McGrath.

As Rose and the Master they both ran along.
'Now I wonder,' says Rose, 'what took you from
　　your home;
You should have stopped there in your Irish
　　demesne,
And not come to gain laurels on Albion's plain.'

'Well, I know,' says McGrath, 'we have wild
　　heather bogs,
But you'll find in old Ireland there's good men
　　and dogs.
Lead on, bold Britannia, give none of your jaw,
Snuff that up your nostrils,' says Master McGrath.

Then the hare she went on just as swift as
    the wind,
He was sometime before her and sometime
    behind.
Rose gave the first turn according to law;
But the second was given by Master McGrath.

The hare she led on with a wonderful view,
And swift as the wind o'er the green field
    she flew.
But he jumped on her back and he held up
    his paw
'Three cheers for old Ireland,' says Master McGrath.

Anonymous

Chorus of Spirits

Gently! – gently! – down! – down!
   From the starry courts on high,
Gently step adown, down
   The ladder of the sky.

Sunbeam steps are strong enough
   For such airy feet:
Spirits, blow your trumpets rough,
   So as they be sweet!

Breathe them loud, the Queen descending,
   Yet a lowly welcome breathe,
Like so many flowerets bending
   Zepher's breezy foot beneath.

George Darley

Astronaut

Give me some information
On China and Greece;
the only place
I ever went was the moon.

Derek.Mahon

Toward Winter

The night is cold on the Great Bog.
The storm is lashing – no small matter.
The sharp wind is laughing at the groans
echoing through the cowering wood.

Anonymous

32

The Meteorite

We crossed the fields by moonlight and by
   moonlight
Counted the whooper swans, each a white
     silhouette,
       A shape from Iceland, and
          picked out thirty, was it,
           Before we were
             interrupted by the
              meteorite
              And its
              reflection
              that among
              the swans
              was lit.

Michael Longley

Starting School

Motherless the first day
she stood alone in the empty schoolyard,
too early for fear of being late.
She stared and shrank
like a startled iris
as the sky exploded.

If she had given in and cried,
lain down on that grey rock
between the specked cliff
and the humpy hill
she might have cried it out,
but the eldest must be strong.

Now, glancing through the kitchen window
or during a summer walk,
a certain texture of stone
with no give in it drives her out
into the raw tundra of dreams.
At the edge of the horizon
between the hill and the speckled cliff
a dry-eyed child sits, frozen.

Mary O'Malley

Girl in a Rope

By the still canal
She enters a slack rope,
Moves, slowly at first, round and round,
Gathering speed,
(Faster, faster now)
She clips the air without a sound –
Swift whirling sight,
Creator of a high design,
Orbiting in sheer delight
The red and white No Parking sign.

Brendan Kennelly

Roisin Dubh

Since last night's star, afar, afar,
    Heaven saw my speed;
I seemed to fly o'er mountains high
    On magic steed.
I dashed through Erne! The world may learn
    The cause from love:
For light or sun shone on me none,
    But Roisin Dubh!

O Roisin mine, droop not, nor pine;
    Look not so dull!
The Pope from Rome shall send thee home
    A pardon full;
The priests are near; O do not fear!
    From heaven above
They come to thee, they come to free
    My Roisin Dubh!

Thee have I loved, for thee have roved
    O'er land and sea;
My heart was sore, and ever more
    It beat for thee;
I could not weep, I could not sleep,
    I could not move!
For night or day, I dreamed alway
    Of Roisin Dubh!

The sea shall burn, the skies shall mourn,
    The skies rain blood,
The world shall rise in dread surprise
    And warful mood,
And hill and lake in Eire shake,
    And hawk turn dove,
Ere you shall pine, ere you decline,
    My Roisin Dubh!

James Clarence Mangan

A Christmas Childhood (part 1)

One side of the potato-pits was white with frost —
How wonderful that was, how wonderful!
And when we put our ears to the paling-post
The music that came out was magical.

The light between the ricks of hay and straw
Was a hole in Heaven's gable. An apple tree
With its December-glinting fruit we saw —
O you, Eve, were the world that tempted me

To eat the knowledge that grew in clay
And death the germ within it! Now and then
I can remember something of the gay
Garden that was childhood's. Again

The tracks of cattle to a drinking-place,
A green stone lying sideways in a ditch
Or any common sight the transfigured face
Of a beauty that the world did not touch.

Patrick Kavanagh

The Song of Wandering Aengus

I went out to the hazel wood,
Because a fire was in my head,
And cut and peeled a hazel wand,
And hooked a berry to a thread;
And when white moths were on the wing,
And moth-like stars were flickering out,
I dropped the berry in a stream
And caught a little silver trout.

When I had laid it on the floor
I went to blow the fire aflame,
But something rustled on the floor,
And some one called me by my name:
It had become a glimmering girl
With apple blossom in her hair
Who called me by my name and ran
And faded through the brightening air.

Though I am old with wandering
Through hollow lands and hilly lands,
I will find out where she has gone,
And kiss her lips and take her hands;
And walk among long dappled grass,
And pluck till time and times are done
The silver apples of
    the moon,
The golden
    apples of
    the sun.

W B Yeats

St Francis and the Birds

When Francis preached love to the birds
They listened, fluttered, throttled up
Into the blue like a flock of words

Released for fun from his holy lips,
Then wheeled back, whirred about his head,
Pirouetted on brothers' capes.

Danced on the wing, for sheer joy played
And sang, like images took flight.
Which was the best poem Francis made,

His argument true, his tone light.

Seamus Heaney

The Fairies

Up the airy mountain,
Down the rushy glen,
We daren't go a-hunting
For fear of little men;
Wee folk, good folk,
Trooping all together;
Green jacket, red cap,
And white owl's feather!

Down along the rocky shore
Some make their home –
They live on crispy pancakes
Of yellow tide-foam;
Some in the reeds
Of the black mountain lake,
With frogs for their watch-dogs,
All night awake.

High on the hilltop
The old king sits;
He is now so old and grey,
He's nigh lost his wits.

With a bridge of white mist
Columbkill he crosses
On his stately journeys
From Slieveleague to Rosses;
Or going up with music
On cold, starry
nights,

To sup with the Queen
Of the gay Northern Lights.

They stole little Bridget
For seven years long;
When she came down again
Her friends were all gone.
They took her lightly back,
Between the night and morrow,
They thought that she
was fast asleep,
But she was dead with sorrow.
They have kept her ever since
Deep within the lake,
On a bed of flag-leaves,
Watching till she wake.

By the craggy hillside,
Through the mosses bare,
They have planted thorn-trees
For pleasure here and there.
Is any man so daring
As dig one up in spite,
He shall find their sharpest thorns
In his bed at night.

Up the airy mountain,
Down the rushy glen,
We daren't go a-hunting
For fear of little men;
Wee folk, good folk,
Trooping all together;
Green jacket,
red cap,
And white
owl's feather!

William Allingham

The Painting

Under the rose-tree's dancing shade
    There stands a little ivory girl,
    Pulling the leaves of pink and pearl
With pale green nails of polished jade.

The red leaves fall upon the mould,
    The white leaves flutter, one by one,
    Down to a blue bowl where the sun,
Like a great dragon, writhes in gold.

The white leaves float upon the air,
    The red leaves flutter idly down,
    Some fall upon her yellow gown,
And some upon her raven hair.

She takes an amber lute and sings,
      And as she sings a silver crane
      Begins his scarlet neck to strain,
And flap his burnished metal wings.

With pale green nails of polished jade,
      Pulling the leaves of pink and pearl,
      There stands a little ivory girl
Under the rose-tree's dancing shade.

Oscar Wilde

from The Village Schoolmaster

Beside yon straggling fence that skirts the way,
With blossom'd furze unprofitably gay,
There, in his noisy mansion, skilled to rule,
The village master taught his little school.
A man severe he was, and stern to view;
I knew him well, and every truant knew:
Well had the boding tremblers learned to trace
The day's disasters in his morning face;
Full well they laughed with counterfeited glee
At all his jokes, for many a joke had he;
Full well the busy whisper circling round
Conveyed the dismal tidings when he frowned.
Yet he was kind, or, if severe in aught,
The love he bore to learning was in fault;
The village all declared how much he knew:
'Twas certain he could write, and cypher too;
Lands he could measure, terms and tides presage,
And e'en the story ran that he could gauge:
In arguing, too, the parson owned his skill;
For e'en though vanquished, he could argue still;

While words of learned length and thundering
    sound
Amazed the gazing rustics ranged around;
And still they gazed, and still the wonder grew,
That one small head could carry all he knew.

But past is all his fame. The very spot
Where many a time he triumphed, is forgot.

Oliver Goldsmith

Johneen

Sure he's five months old, an' he's two foot long,
  Baby Johneen;
Watch yerself now, for he's terrible sthrong,
  Baby Johneen.
An' his fists'll be up if ye make any slips,
He has finger-ends like the daisy-tips.
But he'll have ye attend to the words of his lips,
  Will Johneen.

There's nobody can rightly tell the colour of his eyes,
  This Johneen;
For they're partly o' the earth an' still they're partly o' the skies,
  Like Johneen.
So far as he's thravelled he's been laughin' all the way,
For the little soul is quare an' wise, the little heart is gay;
An' he likes the merry daffodils, he thinks they'd do to play
  With Johneen.

He'll sail a boat yet, if he only has his luck,
    Young Johneen,
For he takes to the wather like any little duck,
    Boy Johneen.
Sure them are the hands now to pull on a rope,
An' nate feet for walkin' the deck on a slope.
But the ship she must wait a wee while yet, I hope,
    For Johneen.

For we couldn't do wantin' him, not just yet,
    Och, Johneen;
'Tis you that are the daisy, an' you that are the pet,
    Wee Johneen.
Here's to your health, an' we'll drink it tonight.
Slainte geal, avic machree! live an' do right.
Slainte geal avourneen! may your days be bright,
    Johneen.

Moira O'Neill

A Poaching Song

When God created water He must have
    thought of fish
And said, 'Let there be salmon to lie on
    Adam's dish!'
So He created Adam, for salmon must be
    caught
And flies too He created, and then of rods
    He thought;
So trees grew straight and slender, and
    Adam learned to fish
And thanked the Lord each evening for
    the brightness on his dish.

But who created bailiffs in a dark hour of
    the night?
Not God, Who loves good fellows and
    taught fish how to bite;
Not God, Who has created the peaceful
    flowing stream.
The salmon ripe for taking when he leaps
    for joy in Spring.

A wise man, Fionn MacCumhaill, caught a
    salmon for his tea
That lived on nuts of knowledge, dropped
    from a knowing tree;
He cooked it and he tasted and knew all men
    could wish
And wise men ever since then sit by a stream
    and fish;
But men unwise and evil, prompted by vicious
    greed,
Forbid good men their pleasure in doing this
    good deed.

Let others praise the herring, the tunny,
    trout or whale,
Give me the noble salmon with lightning in
    his tail;
To monarchs leave the sturgeon, the carp of
    golden hue –
I'll snare the silver salmon, and share the dish
    with you.

Donagh MacDonagh

Brian O'Linn

Brian O'Linn was a gentleman born,
His hair it was long and his beard unshorn,
His teeth were out and his eyes far in –
 'I'm a wonderful beauty,' says Brian O'Linn!

Brian O'Linn was hard up for a coat,
He borrowed the skin of a neighbouring goat,
He buckled the horns right under his chin –
'They'll answer for pistols,' says Brian O'Linn!

Brian O'Linn had no breeches to wear,
He got him a sheepskin to make him a pair,
With the fleshy side out and the woolly side in –
'They are pleasant and cool,' says Brian O'Linn!

Brian O'Linn had no hat to his head,
He stuck on a pot that was under the shed,
He murdered a cod for the sake of his fin –
' 'Twill pass for a feather,' says Brian O'Linn!

Brian O'Linn had no shirt to his back,
He went to a neighbour and borrowed a sack,
He puckered a meal-bag under his chin –
'They'll take it for ruffles,' says Brian O'Linn!

Brian O'Linn had no shoes at all,
He bought an old pair at a cobbler's stall,
The uppers were broke and the soles were thin –
'They'll do me for dancing,' says Brian O'Linn!

Brian O'Linn had no watch to wear,
He bought a fine turnip and scooped it out fair,
He slipped a live cricket right under the skin –
'They'll think it is ticking,' says Brian O'Linn!

Brian O'Linn was in want of a brooch,
He stuck a brass pin in a big cockroach,
The breast of his shirt he fixed it straight in –
'They'll think it's a diamond,' says Brian O'Linn!

Brian O'Linn went a-courting one night,
He set both the mother and daughter to fight –
'Stop, stop,' he exclaimed, 'if you have but the tin,
I'll marry you both,' says Brian O'Linn!

Brian O'Linn went to bring his wife home,
He had but one horse, that was all skin and bone –
'I'll put her behind me, as nate as a pin,
And her mother before me,' says Brian O'Linn!

Brian O'Linn and his wife and wife's mother,
They all crossed over the bridge together,
The bridge broke down, and they all tumbled in –
'We'll go home by water,' says Brian O'Linn!

Anonymous

Biographies

Cecil Frances Alexander (1818-95) Cecil Frances Alexander was born in County Wicklow, but lived in the North of Ireland for most of her life. As a Sunday School teacher in Strabane, she wrote hymns for her pupils and several became famous – All Things Bright and Beautiful, Once in Royal David's City and There is a Green Hill Far Away.

William Allingham (1824-89) Born in Ballyshannon, County Donegal. William Allingham worked as a customs officer while writing his poems at night. Later, he moved to London where he became a friend of Alfred, Lord Tennyson.

Anonymous Any anthology will show you that Anonymous wrote a great number of poems. But sadly, we will never know just who Anonymous was, or indeed were, for anonymous is the word we use when we no longer know who wrote a particular poem. Perhaps the poet was too modest to put his name to the poem or perhaps as the poem was copied out in the years since it was first written, the poet's name has been left out.

Padraic Colum (1881-1972) Born Patrick McCormac Colm in Longford, the son of the workhouse master. He wrote plays for the Irish Theatre but is best remembered as a poet and was an important figure in the Irish Literary Renaissance. He died in the United States where he taught for a while.

George Darley (1795-1846) Born in Dublin and educated at Trinity College. He spent most of his adult life in London where he became a friend of Charles Lamb and Thomas Carlyle. He had an incurable stammer but his poetry flows with great eloquence.

Oliver Goldsmith (1728-74) Born in Pallasmore, County Longford, Oliver Goldsmith was educated at Trinity College, Dublin and in Edinburgh, Scotland. Although he had planned to be a doctor, he seemed unable to settle – at one point he busked his way round Europe playing Irish tunes on his flute. He finally settled in London where he scraped a living as a journalist, and was about to be imprisoned for debt when the manuscript of his novel The Vicar of Wakefield was sold. His most famous poem is The Deserted Village and his play She Stoops to Conquer is still frequently performed.

Eva Gore-Booth (1870-1926) Eva Gore-Booth was born in Lissadell, County Sligo. She was educated at home and then became involved in the Women's Suffrage Movement in England. Eva Gore-Booth published ten books of poetry, but is best known for The Little Waves of Breffny. Her sister was Constance, Countess Markievicz who was very involved in the Easter Rising in Dublin.

Seamus Heaney (1939 -) Born in Castledawson, County Derry, Northern Ireland, Seamus Heaney was educated at Queen's University, Belfast and then went on to teach at the University of California, Harvard University and Oxford University in England where he was Professor of Poetry from 1989 to 1994. He has produced many collections of verse and translations of well-known works and his translation of the epic poem, Beowulf, won him the Whitbread Book of the Year Award in 1999. He was awarded the Nobel Prize for Literature in 1995.

Robert Dwyer Joyce (1830-83) Robert Dwyer Joyce was born in Glenosheen, County Limerick. He trained first as a teacher and later became a professor of English. He also qualified as a doctor and in 1866 emigrated to Boston, where he continued to write. In 1872, he published Ballads of Irish Chivalry and in 1876, the epic poem Deirdre. He returned to Ireland shortly before he died.

Patrick Kavanagh (1904-67) Born in Iniskeen, County Monaghan, Patrick Joseph Kavanagh worked as a farmer until he went to live in Dublin in 1939 where he became a writer and journalist. Today he is widely regarded as one of Ireland's finest poets. He is particularly famous for his poem The Great Hunger which was published in 1942 and is a long and passionate account of the harsh life of an Irish farmer.

Brendan Kennelly (1936 -) Brendan Kennelly was born in Ballylongford, County Kerry and educated at Trinity College, Dublin where he became Professor of Modern Literature. He has had over 30 collections of poetry, five plays and two novels published, and edited the Penguin Book of Irish Verse.

Francis Ledwidge (1891-1917) Born in Slane, County Meath, Francis Ledwidge worked as a farm labourer and was greatly encouraged in his writing of poetry by his local landlord, Lord Dunsany. His writing has been compared to the Scottish poet, Robert Burns and to the English poet, John Clare, both of who wrote about the countryside. Ledwidge was killed in the First World War, at Flanders in Belgium.

Michael Longley (1939 -) Educated in Belfast and Dublin, Michael Longley worked first as a schoolmaster. He has written several collections of poetry and later works include Gorse Fires (1991) and The Weather in Japan (2000), both of which won him literary prizes. In April 2001, he won The Queen's Gold Medal for Poetry.

Donagh MacDonagh (1912 – 68) The son of the poet and patriot, Thomas MacDonagh, Donagh MacDonagh was born in Dublin. He was orphaned after his father's execution in 1916 following the Easter Rising and his mother's drowning in 1917. Educated at University College, Dublin, he became a barrister in 1935 and a judge in 1941. He published plays and poetry collections and was co-editor of The Oxford Book of Irish Verse.

Derek Mahon (1941 -) Derek Mahon was born in Belfast and educated at Trinity College, Dublin. He was first a teacher, then a journalist, and then turned to writing poetry. With Seamus Heaney and Michael Longley, he was involved in the 1960s with the Northern Poets, a poetry workshop in Belfast. Poems 1962-1978 appeared in 1979 and a new Selected Poems was published in 1991.

James Clarence Mangan (1803 - 49) Born in Dublin but with no formal education and always poor and in ill health, James Mangan mastered several languages and worked in Trinity College. He would walk round Dublin wearing a voluminous cloak, green spectacles and a pointed hat. He wrote many great poems and was highly regarded by Yeats and Joyce. He died of cholera in the Meath Hospital, Dublin.

Adelaide O'Keeffe (1776 - 1855) Adelaide O'Keeffe was the only daughter of John O'Keeffe, an Irish playwright who became blind in 1790. While she looked after him, Adelaide wrote several books of children's poetry.

Mary O'Malley (1954 -) Mary O'Malley was born in Connemara and educated at University College, Galway. A Hennessy Award winner, she has published plays and four collections of poetry, the most recent in 2001, Asylum Road. She has written for radio and television and often broadcasts. She travels and lectures in Europe and the US.

Moira O'Neill (1870 -?) Moira O'Neill was the pen name of Agnes Higginson Skrine. She wrote Songs from the Glens of Antrim which was published in 1900 but otherwise, little is known about her.

Patrick Pearse (1879 - 1916) Patrick Pearse was born in Dublin, and studied to become a barrister but practised only briefly. From an early age, he was deeply interested in Irish cultural life, especially the language, and he wrote plays and poetry in Irish and English. A patriot and revolutionary, he was executed with his brother Willie in the Easter Rising.

Jonathan Swift (1667-1745) Jonathan Swift was born in Dublin. He is acknowledged as the greatest satirist in the English language, and is best remembered as the author of Gulliver's Travels, which was the only writing for which he was ever paid (£200) as everything else was published anonymously. In 1713 he became Dean of St Patrick's Cathedral in Dublin.

Oscar Wilde (1854-1900) A brilliant playwright, novelist and poet, Oscar Wilde was born in Dublin and was famous for his wit and dazzling style. He also wrote a collection of fairy tales for his two sons. Once, when stopped by a customs official, he is famously reported to have stated, 'I have nothing to declare except my genius.'

WB Yeats (1865-1939) William Butler Yeats was born in Dublin and studied at the School of Art but gave up art for the study of literature. Much of his writing is taken up with Irish history and politics along with folklore. In 1923, he received the Nobel Prize for Literature.